MAR   2016

D0570907

FAST FACTS

Awesome Knights

KINGFISHER
NEW YORK

KINGFISHER
LONDON & NEW YORK

Copyright © Macmillan Publishers International Ltd 2016
Published in the United States by Kingfisher,
175 Fifth Ave., New York, NY 10010
Kingfisher is an imprint of Macmillan Children's Books, London
All rights reserved.

Distributed in the U.S. and Canada by Macmillan,
175 Fifth Ave., New York, NY 10010

Library of Congress Cataloging-in-Publication data
has been applied for.

Interior design by Tall Tree Ltd
Cover design by Peter Clayman

Adapted from an original text by Claire Llewellyn
Literacy consultants: Kerenza Ghosh, Stephanie Laird

Illustration by Steve Stone (represented by Artist Partners Ltd)
with addtional artwork by Thomas Bayley and Lee Gibbons

ISBN 978-0-7534-7252-1 (HB)
ISBN 978-0-7534-7247-7 (PB)

Kingfisher books are available for special promotions
and premiums. For details contact: Special Markets
Department, Macmillan, 175 Fifth Ave.,
New York, NY 10010.

For more information, please visit
www.kingfisherbooks.com

Printed in China
9 8 7 6 5 4 3 2 1
1TR/1115/WKT/UG/128MA

Picture credits
The Publisher would like to thank the following for permission to reproduce their material.
Top = t; Bottom = b; Center = c; Left = l; Right = r
Front Cover Shutterstock/Grisha Bruev; Back cover Shutterstock/Ancher; 1c Heritage Image Partnership/Royal Armouries; 4–5 Getty Images David Tomlinson; 5 With the Kind Permission of Warwick Castle; 6bl Bridgeman Art Library, The Ashmolean Museum, Oxford; The British Museum; 7lb Heritage Image Partnership The Royal Armouries; 7tr Heritage Image Partnership The Royal Armouries; 6–7b Corbis Barry Lewis; 14cl Alamy/ E. Katie Holm; 14cl Alamy/Jim Cole; 14r Alamy/David White; 14bl Alamy/Kari Niemelainen; 14bl Alamy/ Eric Nathan; 15cl Alamy/Fabrice Bettex; 15b Alamy/Marina Spironetti; 15b Alamy/Eric Nathan; 16br With the Kind Permission of Warwick Castle; 16cr Dorling Kindersley; 17t Corbis/Michel Setboun; 17b Heritage Image Partnership The British Library; 18–19 Art Archive/University Library Prague/Alfredo Dagli Orti; 19tr Corbis/ The Gallery Collection; 20l Corbis/Darama/zefa; 20cl Heritage Image Partnership/The Print Collector; 20bl Heritage Image Partnership/Royal Armouries; 21tl Heritage Image Partnership/Royal Armouries; 21bl Heritage Image Partnership/Royal Armouries; 21br Heritage Image Partnership/Royal Armouries; 21background Corbis/Mimmo Jodice; 26cr Art Archive/Musée Condé Chantilly/Gianni Dagli Orti; 28l Corbis/ Dave Bartruff; 28c AKG, London, 28br AKG, London; 29l Art Archive/Musée Condé Chantilly/Gianni Dagli Orti; 29tr Bridgeman Art Library/British Museum; 29surround Alamy/MEPL; 31br Heritage Image Partnership/Royal Armouries.

CE
Common era, or Christian era.
The period of time since the
birth of Jesus Christ.

Contents

NO LONGER PROPERTY OF
KING COUNTY LIBRARY SYSTEM

Middle Ages
The period from the fall of
the Roman Empire in 476CE
until about 1500.

A double-edged
longsword was
often used by a
knight to bring
down his enemy.

Knights
and castles

A knight was a noble armored warrior who fought
on horseback during the Middle Ages. He served
his lord in battle and defended his lord's castle—
a stone fortified building that protected a town or
a region. Castles were used both as private homes
and as military bases for knights.

Loarre Castle in Aragon, an old kingdom in Spain, was built between about 1020 and the 1200s.

TOP FIVE BITESIZE FACTS

The first castles were built from wood.

A ditch surrounding a castle is called a moat.

Windsor Castle, just outside London, is the oldest and largest inhabited castle in the world.

There are about 1500 castle sites in Britain, of which only 300 are still standing.

The largest castle in the world is Prague Castle, which is big enough to fit 13 soccer fields.

Age of knights

Some knights became powerful and famous, as loyal friends or as fierce enemies, as champions of the king— or even as **traitors**.

Knights carried banners displaying their **coat of arms**. The coat of arms represented the knight's noble family name, so his opponent would know who he is.

First knights

The first knights were lightly armed and could attack quickly on horseback, as cavalry. But more heavily armored warriors were also used to smash through enemy lines, and during the Middle Ages this type of attack became important in battle. These knights were armed with swords and protected by helmets.

crossguard

A firm footing

A stirrup holds a horseman steady in the saddle, making it easier for him to swing a sword in battle. The stirrup was invented in Asia and by the 700s it was being used throughout Europe. This one invention changed warfare forever.

This bronze stirrup was made in Asia more than 1300 years ago.

Rise of the knight

The age of the European knights began in the early 900s, when local lords and their mounted warriors defended people from raiders. Knights fought with swords, axes, and long spears called **lances**. Some knights also carried clubs with spiky metal heads, called maces.

The ball at the end of the handle on this broadsword is called the pommel.

cavalry
Soldiers who attack on horseback. In the Middle Ages, cavalry was the fastest type of military force.

Mask of metal

In about 600CE, most fighting men wore simple helmets, but this **Anglo-Saxon** helmet was fit for a king. It is decorated with pictures of battles and it has eyebrows, a nose, and a mustache. A crest runs over the top of the helmet and it has two dragon heads with red gemstones for eyes.

A replica of a ceremonial helmet from England in the early 600s.

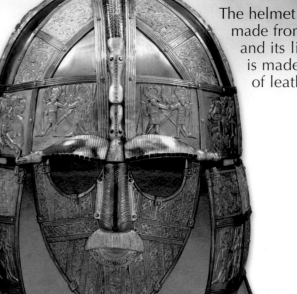

The helmet is made from iron and its lining is made of leather.

iron with silver pattern

Elite weapons

This rare, decorated ax was made in the 600s. It was made by a tribe of people called the Franks who lived in what is now Germany. During the age of the knights, however, the sword was the most important weapon of a knight, and a symbol of his status.

The groove running down the middle of the blade is called the fuller, or "blood gutter."

TOP FIVE BITESIZE FACTS

A knight's **broadsword** could be up to 45 inches (115 centimeters) long, and was heavy.

A greatsword was even longer—it was so long that a knight needed both hands to use it.

The sword's pommel sometimes held a small badge showing the knight's coat of arms.

Knights would often carry a broadsword, a smaller sword for thrusting, and a dagger.

The dagger could pierce gaps between armor.

7

Labels on upper-left image:

chain-mail hood, or coif

helmet with a nose bar

The men of mail

The Normans were a warlike people from northern France who were descended from the **Vikings**. In the 1000s and 1100s, they invaded southern Italy and England, where they built many castles.

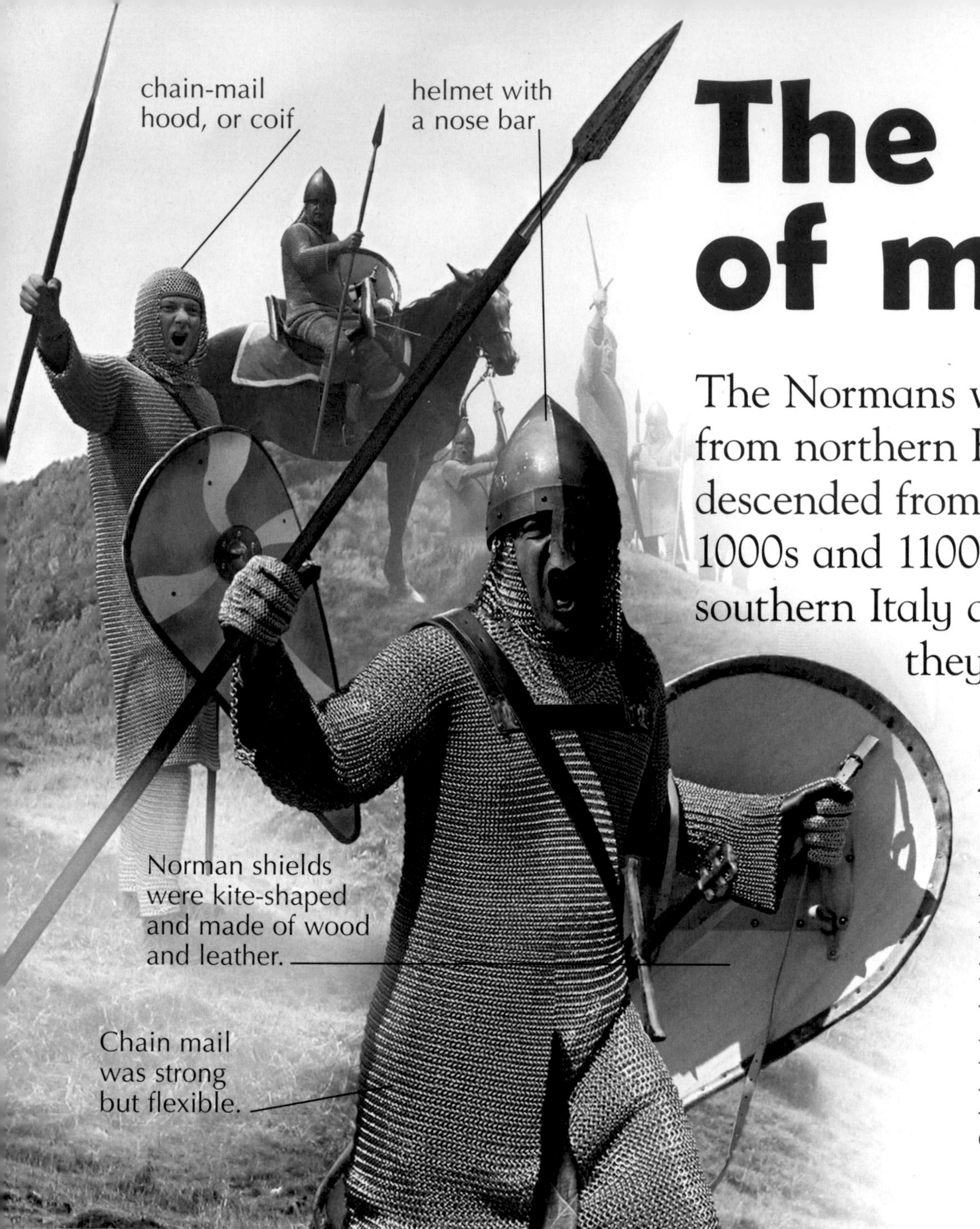

Norman shields were kite-shaped and made of wood and leather.

Chain mail was strong but flexible.

Chain mail

The Norman knights wore a chain-mail coat called a hauberk. To make this, thick iron wire was shaped into rings. Each ring was linked with four others. The hauberk was worn over a padded tunic and leggings called chausses.

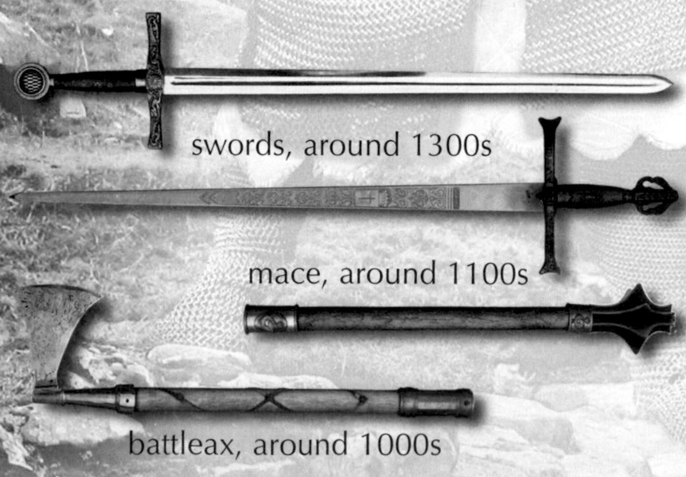

swords, around 1300s

mace, around 1100s

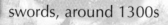

battleax, around 1000s

Weapons of war

In the 1000s, swords were mostly used for slashing and cutting. By the late 1200s, swords were being made to pierce through chain mail. A blow from a mace or from a **battleax** could also break through chain mail. Knights had to use shields as their main defense.

chain mail
Armor made from iron rings that are linked together.

An armored glove was called a gauntlet.

The great helm covered the whole head and was padded on the inside.

The hauberk weighed about 22 pounds (10 kilograms)—almost as much as four bricks.

The great helm

In the year 1250, European knights were still wearing chain-mail armor. Over the hauberk, they now wore a cloth tunic called a **surcoat**. Instead of the simple helmet with a nose bar, some knights now wore the great helm, which looked like a pail with eye slits.

TOP FIVE BITESIZE FACTS

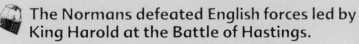

- The Normans, led by William, Duke of Normandy, invaded England in 1066.

- The Normans defeated English forces led by King Harold at the Battle of Hastings.

- The story of the invasion is shown in a **tapestry** called the Bayeux Tapestry.

- The name "Norman" comes from "Norsemen," meaning "men from the north."

- Norman knights carried their horses to England in ships.

The Crusades

In 1095, Christian knights from western Europe traveled to fight the Muslims, or Saracens, living in the **Holy Land**. This region is now occupied by Syria, Israel, Lebanon, Palestine, and Egypt. The wars that followed are called the Crusades, or "wars of the cross."

Saracens fought with a sword and round shield. They also used bows and arrows.

Crusader steel

Weapons included straight swords and falchions—a curved sword with one cutting edge. Knights also used flails—sticks with spiked balls. Some helmets of the 1200s were flat-topped. Others had rounded caps.

sword, early 1300s

falchion, 1200s

lance, around 1100s

flail, 1500s

helmet, around 1200s

Crusades
Military expeditions by medieval Christians to try and capture the Holy Land from the Muslims.

Held for ransom

As armored knights battled in the heat and dust, cities were conquered and civilians were killed. If captured, a knight was sometimes held prisoner until a **ransom** was paid for his release.

Krak des Chevaliers in Syria was one of the strongest castles built by the Crusaders.

Crusader knights usually wore a cross on their tunic and shield to show they were Christians.

TOP FIVE BITESIZE FACTS

- Crusader knights even attacked other Christians. They ransacked the city of Constantinople (Istanbul) in 1204.

- The Crusaders left the Holy Land in 1291.

- There were nine major Crusades in total.

- Crusader knights formed religious groups, or orders, such as the **Knights Templar**.

- In 1212, thousands of children from France and Germany sailed to the Holy Land in the Children's Crusade—they were never seen again.

Homes of stone

By the 1100s, stone castles had replaced early wooden structures and round towers had replaced square ones. The **keep**, or stronghold, was surrounded by huge walls and sometimes by a **moat** full of water, crossed by a drawbridge.

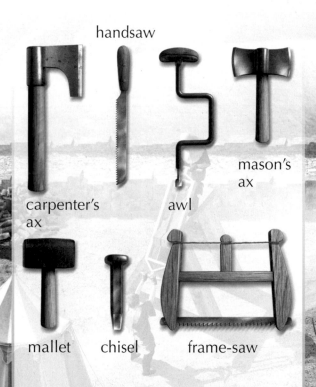

handsaw

carpenter's ax

awl

mason's ax

mallet

chisel

frame-saw

Wooden scaffolding helped the stonemasons to build the gatehouse.

This crane was powered by a worker walking inside a treadwheel.

Tools of the trade
Medieval craftsmen used basic metal tools and muscle power. Carpenters sawed and hammered, while masons chiseled the stone and checked that the walls were strong and straight.

Roof tiles were made from slate (shown here) or ceramic (baked clay).

TOP FIVE BITESIZE FACTS

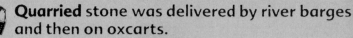

- **Quarried** stone was delivered by river barges and then on oxcarts.

- Stones were held together using a cement made from sand, lime, and water.

- Castle walls could be 33 feet (10 meters) thick —about half the length of a bowling lane.

- The tops of the walls were called **battlements**, from where defenders could shoot missiles.

- A spiked metal barrier called a **portcullis** could be lowered by chains to protect the castle's thick main door.

The battlements had low **embrasures** and high **merlons**, so that archers could fire or take cover.

drawbridge

A bridge over a castle moat that could be raised to stop enemies entering the castle.

13

Castle life

steward
The person in charge of managing the castle.

A castle was not just a **fortress**, it was a home for many people. The castle of a lord would also be occupied by the lord's family, his squires (trainee knights), and his servants.

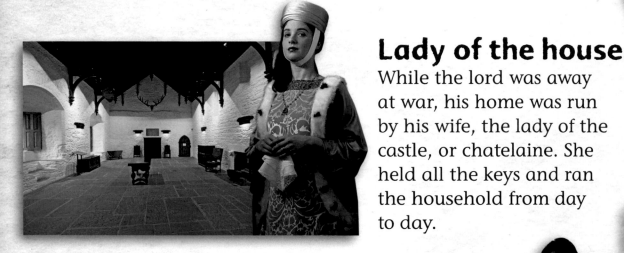

Lady of the house

While the lord was away at war, his home was run by his wife, the lady of the castle, or chatelaine. She held all the keys and ran the household from day to day.

Castle chapel

The castle had its own chapel, a tall chamber with stained-glass windows. The walls were decorated with stories from the Bible. In front of the altar, the priest led the prayers for the castle household and knights prayed here before battle.

prison

store-room

chapel

Blacksmith

In a corner of the courtyard, a blacksmith hammered away at his **anvil**. He used it to make and repair iron tools, weapons, chains, wheel rims, and horseshoes.

KEY

lower levels

first floor

second floor

great hall

kitchen

courtyard

Round towers
required spiral
staircases made of
stone. These were
easy to defend.

work-
shop

solar

lord's bedroom

toilet

TOP FIVE BITESIZE FACTS

 Other people living in the castle included the steward, soldiers, servants, and cooks.

The solar was a private living room on the second floor.

The toilet was called the garderobe.

The garderobe had a stone seat and a long shaft that dropped down to a sewage pit.

The castle's **spiral staircases** all turned clockwise. This made it hard for attackers coming up the stairs to use their sword arms.

Changing times

The first castles were built for defense and they were not very comfortable. By the 1400s, rich **nobles** wanted more luxurious homes, so some were turned into splendid buildings called palaces.

Lack of comfort

The castle rooms had little furniture. Linen, clothes, and valuable goods were kept in big chests. The four-poster bed had drapes to keep out drafts.

Great hall

The center of activity in many castles was the great hall. This was a lofty room with tall windows and a high, wooden roof. Its walls were hung with tapestries, and the floor covered with sweet-smelling rushes. Logs would burn in a huge fireplace but the hall could be cold and drafty in winter.

TOP FIVE BITESIZE FACTS

- People in the Middle Ages ate off wooden plates or slabs of bread called trenchers.

- By the 1400s, good table manners had become an important part of castle dining.

- One of the most precious items in the great hall was the salt cellar.

- The salt cellar was placed in front of the lord's most important guest at dinner.

- Musicians in the minstrels' gallery entertained the nobles, knights, and other guests.

Heart of the castle

Today, the great hall of this English castle displays suits of armor and old weapons. In the Middle Ages, the halls were not just places to entertain with feasts and music. They also served as places for meetings between a lord and his knights to discuss battles. The great hall was also used to put criminals on trial.

From the kitchen

A noble banquet might include enormous pies, fine white bread rolls, roasted swan, or wild boar. Meat was cooked in pots or roasted on spits. Ordinary people ate simple food, such as crusts of rough bread, cheese, broth, or oatmeal.

roast pheasants and sauce

great hall of Warwick Castle, England

Great banquets

A **high table** for nobles, knights, and royal guests stood at one end of the great hall, covered with fine linen. It was laid with silver cups, plates, spoons, and knives. In the lower part of the hall, people sat on benches and ate off a wooden board.

This famous "round table" has been hung on the wall of the great hall in Winchester Castle, England. It is painted with the names of the knights of the mythical King Arthur.

An English duke called John of Gaunt (1340–1399) is shown here feasting with the King of Portugal and four bishops.

17

Castle towns and lands

Many medieval castles were built on the site of **ancient strongholds**, where towns had already developed over the ages. In conquered lands, castles were built on new sites and new towns were built next to them.

Town charters

New towns were allowed by the king in a document called a charter, which was sealed with wax. This seal, from about 1316, is from Conwy, a walled castle town in northern Wales.

edible snails for sale

butcher chopping venison (deer meat)

A walled city

The city of Carcassonne in southwestern France has been a castle town since the days of the Celts and the Romans. Its large defenses include double walls and 53 towers. The town was the scene of religious turmoil and warfare for hundreds of years.

fortify
To defend or make something strong against attackers.

Market day

Castle towns had busy streets with shops and market stalls selling food, woolen cloth, or leather goods. There were blacksmiths, barrel-makers, and wheelwrights, who made and repaired wheels. There were inns selling ale and wine, where travelers could rest and stable their horses.

Fruits of labor

The lands around the castle were governed by the lord of the castle, and **taxes** were paid to him. The lord also owned the watermills or windmills, which ground the wheat or barley. Farmers and laborers had to give food to the castle and the church.

fishmonger and barrel

TOP FIVE BITESIZE FACTS

- Castle towns were surrounded by high walls and strong gatehouses that joined to the castle defenses.

- The lord of the castle earned money by taxing the people working in the town.

- During a war, knights often became rich by looting or pillaging towns.

- The medieval market at Norwich, England, had 130 different trades in the 1200s.

- Large markets, or fairs, would also have entertainers, such as musicians, acrobats, stilt walkers, and fools.

The men of plate

Chain-mail armor could be pierced by a well-aimed arrow or a spear. After 1220, knights began to use a new type of armor. They protected parts of their body with plates of solid steel.

Metal workers

Here, an **armorer** hammers away in his workshop. Each city made armor with its own mark. Famous armorer towns included Milan in Italy, and Augsburg and Nuremberg in Germany. The most expensive plate armor was specially made to fit the wearer.

TOP FIVE BITESIZE FACTS

 The first plate armor covered only some parts of the body. By the 1400s, whole suits of armor were made covering everything.

 The steel plates were joined with leather straps, which allowed easier movement.

A suit of armor was called a harness.

 Some suits could weigh 110 pounds (50 kilograms).

A knight was armed by his squire, who dressed him from the feet upward.

shirt of
chain mail

gauntlet

cuisse

poleyn

greave

solleret

This knight is
wearing armor dating
from around 1475.
His horse would
have had its own
plate armor.

Gauntlet

The first knights
protected their hands
with long chain-mail sleeves. From the
1300s, jointed plates were used to cover
the hands, with metal cuffs over the
wrists. This armor, called a gauntlet, was
worn over a leather glove.

Knights in shining armor

By the 1400s, plate armor gave the best
protection for a knight. The finest suits
of armor, or harnesses, were made for
kings and princes, and they cost a
fortune. However, even these could be
pierced by a bolt fired from a crossbow
or battered by blows from a sword.

pauldron

bevor

plate armor
Protective suit made of
metal plates.

Battle!

Knights thundered into battle on huge warhorses. They aimed to knock the enemy knights from their saddles using lances, and then attack them with swords and maces. **Foot soldiers** tried to dismount knights with **pikes**.

Mud and blood

Battles soon became chaotic hand-to-hand fights. Victory was often decided by the weather—rain turned fields into mud causing armor to sink. This scene recreates the Battle of Poitiers, fought between England and France in the Hundred Years' War.

TOP FIVE **BITESIZE** FACTS

 Defending troops would put up wooden stakes called palings to stop enemy cavalry.

 Archers used longbows to create a hail of arrows to pierce a knight's plate armor.

 A longbow could fire an arrow more than 980 feet (300 meters).

 The Hundred Years' War actually lasted from 1337 to 1453.

 The Battle of Poitiers ended with an English victory and the capture of the French king.

caltrop with four spikes

Spikes called caltrops were laid on the battlefield to injure the enemy's horses.

longbow

A large, light bow that could shoot an arrow over long distances.

23

Sieges

To win control of a region, an army had to capture its castles. Knights and other soldiers surrounded the walls and cut off all supplies and support. The aim was to force the enemy to surrender.

All-out assault

These attackers have stripped the countryside bare of food. They now launch a final attack with huge catapults, battering rams, and siege towers. Arrows rain down on the castle.

mangonel

trebuchet

Various types of catapult were used to throw missiles at the walls or over the battlements. Cannons did not come into use until the 1340s.

TOP FIVE BITESIZE FACTS

- Attackers would dig tunnels under walls in order to make the walls collapse.

- Siege towers were nicknamed belfries, because they looked like the bell tower of a church.

- A mangonel was a type of catapult that hurled rocks from a cup at the end of its arm.

- A trebuchet used a big weight to hurl rocks.

- Attacking soldiers stood behind a protective wall called a pavise.

siege tower

siege
The attack of a castle or city by surrounding it, often cutting it off from supplies of food and water.

scaling ladder

Gatehouse defense
Portcullises were grids of timber and iron that were lowered to trap enemy troops inside the gatehouse. There, they would meet a hail of arrows, crossbow bolts, or spears. Rocks, boiling water, or even heated sand could be dropped onto the attackers through openings known as meurtrièrs, or murder-holes.

Tournaments

Knights needed to practice their fighting skills. Mock battles, or *mêlées*, were held as well as bouts of single combat, known as jousting. Large fighting festivals, called tournaments, became very popular.

For the ladies

A knight might dedicate his jousting contest to a lady of the court seated in the stands. He would have been identified by his coat of arms.

jousting
A competition between two knights on horseback who were usually armed with lances.

At full tilt

In the 1400s, a type of jousting called tilting became fashionable. Knights on horses, separated by a fence, raced toward each other, aiming to dismount their opponent. Lances had blunt tips, but injuries could still be bad, so padded helmets and strong armor were worn.

TOP FIVE BITESIZE FACTS

- A jousting lance could be 13 feet (four meters) long.

- During a joust, the lance was held in the couched position—close to the knight's body and tucked underneath the arm.

- The disc in front of the hand on a lance was called the vamplate.

- In 1559, French king Henry II was killed by accident during a joust.

- Other weapons used in a joust included swords, daggers, and maces.

The code of honor

From the 1100s onward, knights across Europe were expected to behave honorably and to follow Christian teachings. They were supposed to be courteous, gentle, and noble, and to protect the weak from the strong.

The Black Prince

Edward the Black Prince (1330–1376) was named after the color of his armor. The son of the English king, he was famous for his chivalry in battle, treating enemy knights with respect.

tomb statue of the Black Prince

Page to squire

At about seven years old, a boy was sent to a castle to serve as a page. He would learn good manners and fighting skills. When he was about 14, he could become a squire, helping a knight on and off the battlefield. Once he had proved himself in battle, he could become a knight.

A French knight of the 1300s is armed by his squire.

"Dubbing" a knight

When a king made a man into a knight he tapped a sword on each of the man's shoulders—an act called dubbing. This signified his knighthood.

In love with love

Knights were in love with the idea of love. Poets were always writing about knights who honored a pure, noble lady with little hope of winning her affection. This "fine" or "courtly" love had little to do with real, passionate love.

Love— or death!

This shield was made in the 1400s. It shows a young knight declaring his love for his lady. He swears that if she rejects his love, the figure of Death (behind the knight) will carry him away.

A noble lady is seated in her castle.

A knight kneels before her, pledging his service.

chivalry
The ideal virtues of the knight, such as courage, honor, respect, generosity, and courtesy.

TOP FIVE BITESIZE FACTS

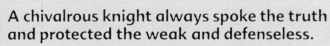

- A dubbing ceremony would be held after the knight had spent a night praying in a chapel.
- The knights' code was called chivalry.
- A chivalrous knight always spoke the truth and protected the weak and defenseless.
- He also never turned his back on an enemy.
- The age of chivalry ended by the 1500s when knights had been replaced by infantrymen and cannons.

Glossary

ancient stronghold
A historical place that has been fortified against attack. Castles often stand on the sites of more ancient forts.

Anglo-Saxon
Germanic peoples who invaded England from the 400s.

anvil
A heavy iron block on which hot metal is hammered into shape by a blacksmith.

armorer
In the Middle Ages, a person skilled in forging weapons and plate armor from iron and steel.

battleax
A large, broad-bladed ax used in battles of the Middle Ages.

battlements
The upper part of a fortified wall.

broadsword
A long sword with a wide blade.

coat of arms
An image representing a knight's family name, often shown on a shield.

embrasure
A low section of a castle's battlements through which an archer can shoot.

foot soldiers
Soldiers who do not fight on horseback. They are supported by archers.

fortress
A defensive building designed as a military base rather than a private home.

high table
In a castle, the lord's table, which is on a platform at the end of the great hall.

Holy Land
Those lands of western Asia held to be sacred by Jews, Christians, and Muslims.

keep
A castle's central tower, with thick walls.

Knights Templar
A specially chosen group of warrior-monks who became powerful during the Crusades.

lance
A type of long spear, used by knights when charging on horseback.

medieval
Dating from the Middle Ages.

merlon

A high section of a castle's battlements that provides cover for an archer.

moat

A water-filled trench surrounding a castle.

noble

A person of the highest social class.

pike

A long spear used by foot soldiers against cavalry in the 1400s.

portcullis

A heavy grid of timber and iron.

quarried

Cut from a quarry of rocks. Quarried stone was transported to the site of a castle, where it was used to build walls.

ransom

Money demanded for the release of a prisoner.

spiral staircase

A winding staircase inside a castle tower.

surcoat

A cloth tunic worn over armor. During the Crusades, a surcoat stopped metal armor from overheating in the sun.

tapestry

A handwoven textile featuring patterns or pictures, used as wall hangings in many old castles.

taxes

Money or goods that must be paid to those governing the land.

traitor

Someone who breaks an agreement, betraying his or her loyalty.

Vikings

Medieval warriors from Denmark, Sweden, or Norway. The Normans were descendants of the Vikings who lived in northern France.

Index